Supposing Stories

At the Park, At School and At Home

Lucia King

INDIA · SINGAPORE · MALAYSIA

ISBN
Paperback 979-8-89277-580-9
Hardcase 979-8-89415-987-4

THIS BOOK BELONGS TO ....

Dedicated To

Shanaya

Acknowledgements

I am thankful to Sudhir, who lent me a patient ear, immense support and some great suggestions throughout this journey.

I would like to thank Sandesh as well, who inspired me to become an Author.

Thanks also to the Notion Press team who helped me transform my dream into a reality.

The Illustrator acknowledges the use of GenCraft to create and modify the images used for this book.

At the Park

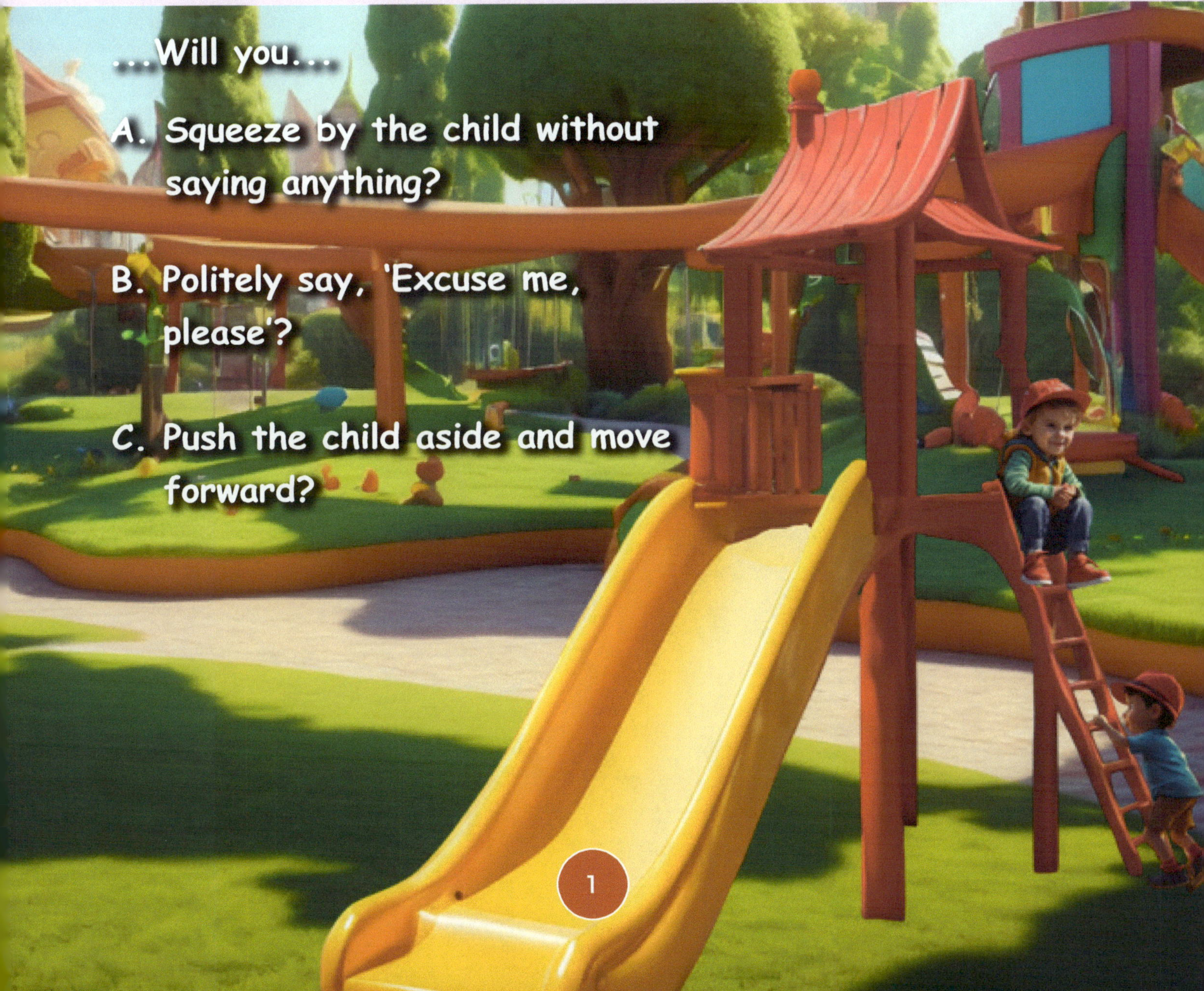

Supposing you wish to play on the slide and are about to climb up the ladder. However, another child is in your way...

The best thing to do is to
politely say, "Excuse me, please."
It is never okay to push
another child.

2

Supposing you climb up and are ready to slide down, and you see that another child is sitting at the end of the slide,

The best thing to do is to say politely, "Please move, I need to slide down."

It's always good to check that the slide is clear before starting.

Supposing you are playing in the garden, and your friend joins you. He has a lollipop in his mouth. Your friend knows you love lollipops and offers you the same one that he has been licking,

The best thing to do is to say politely,
"Sorry, lollipops should not be shared."
It is good NOT to share lollipops.
6

Supposing you are playing in the park with your friends, and one of them falls down,

Would you...

A. Say politely, 'Are you okay? Do you need help?'

B. Start laughing loudly at them?

C. Ignore them and continue playing.

The best thing to do is to
ask politely, "Are you okay?
Do you need help?"

Be kind to everyone and
show concern.

8

Supposing you are playing in the park with your friends, and a stranger walks up to you and offers you something delicious to eat, like sweets, chocolates, toffees,

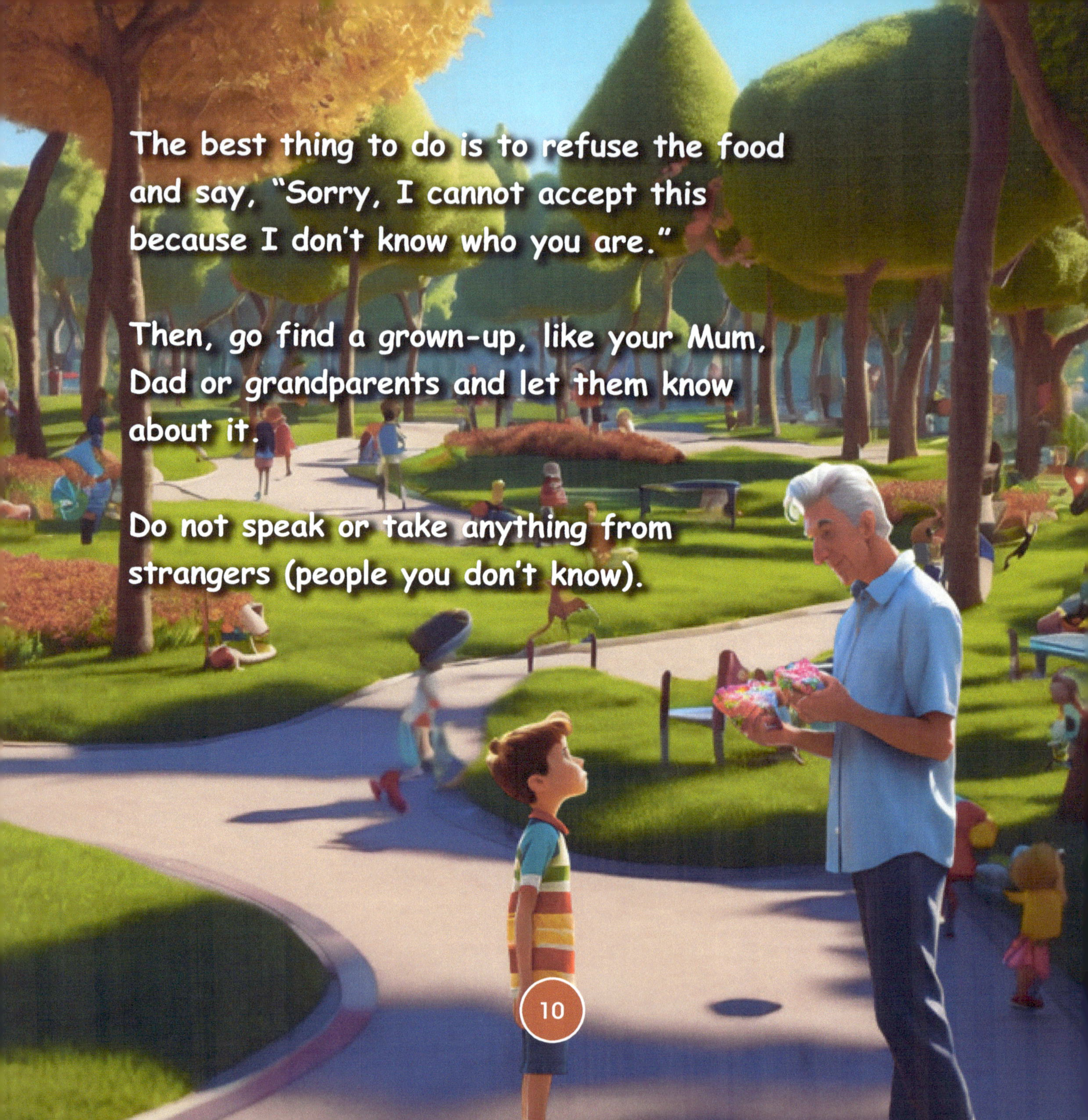

The best thing to do is to refuse the food and say, "Sorry, I cannot accept this because I don't know who you are."

Then, go find a grown-up, like your Mum, Dad or grandparents and let them know about it.

Do not speak or take anything from strangers (people you don't know).

Supposing you are playing on the swing in the park, and your parent is pushing the swing back and forth. Suddenly, you feel like getting off,

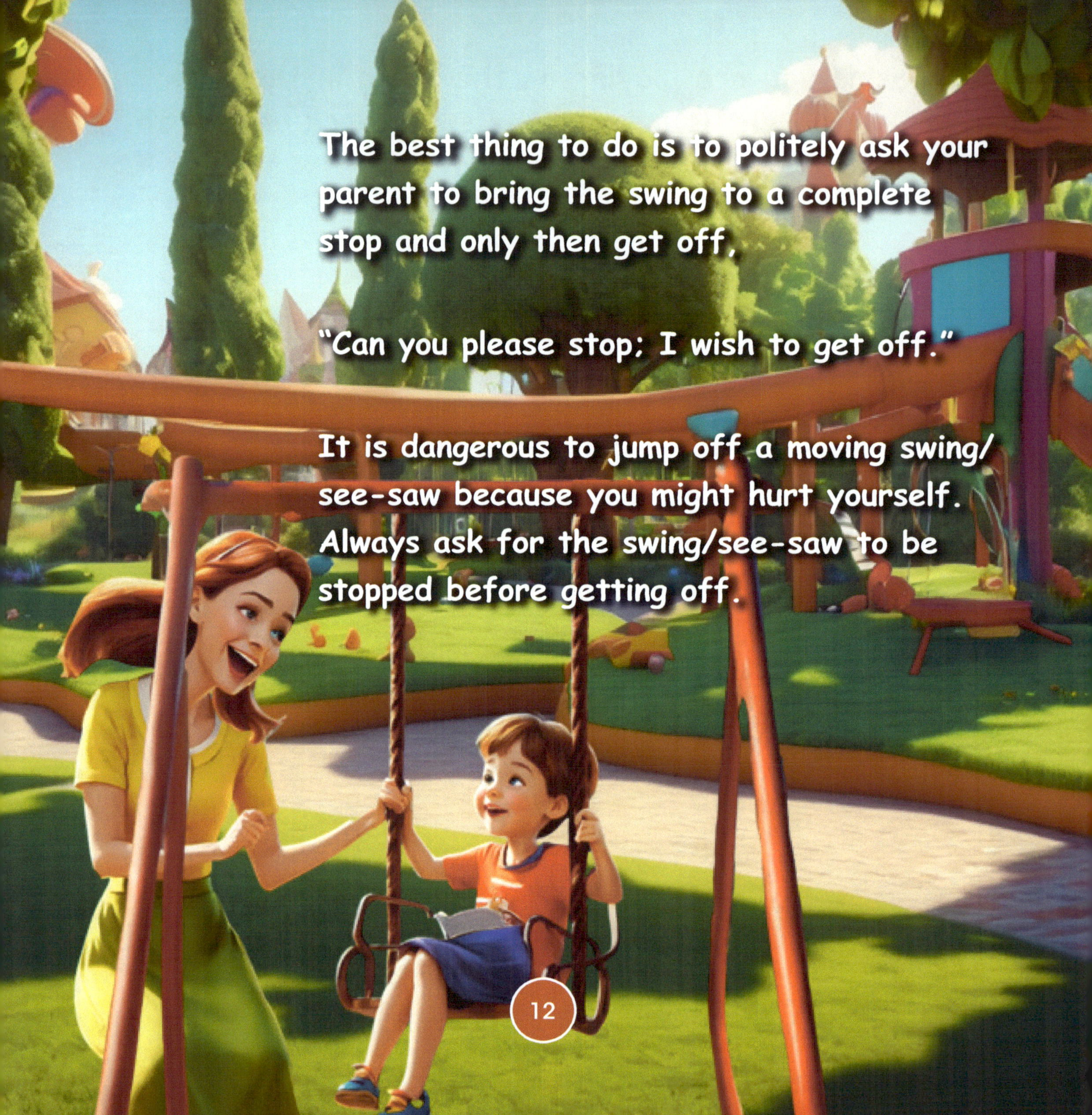

The best thing to do is to politely ask your parent to bring the swing to a complete stop and only then get off.

"Can you please stop; I wish to get off."

It is dangerous to jump off a moving swing/see-saw because you might hurt yourself. Always ask for the swing/see-saw to be stopped before getting off.

Supposing you wish to use the animal rocker at the Park. When you get to it, another child is already using it,

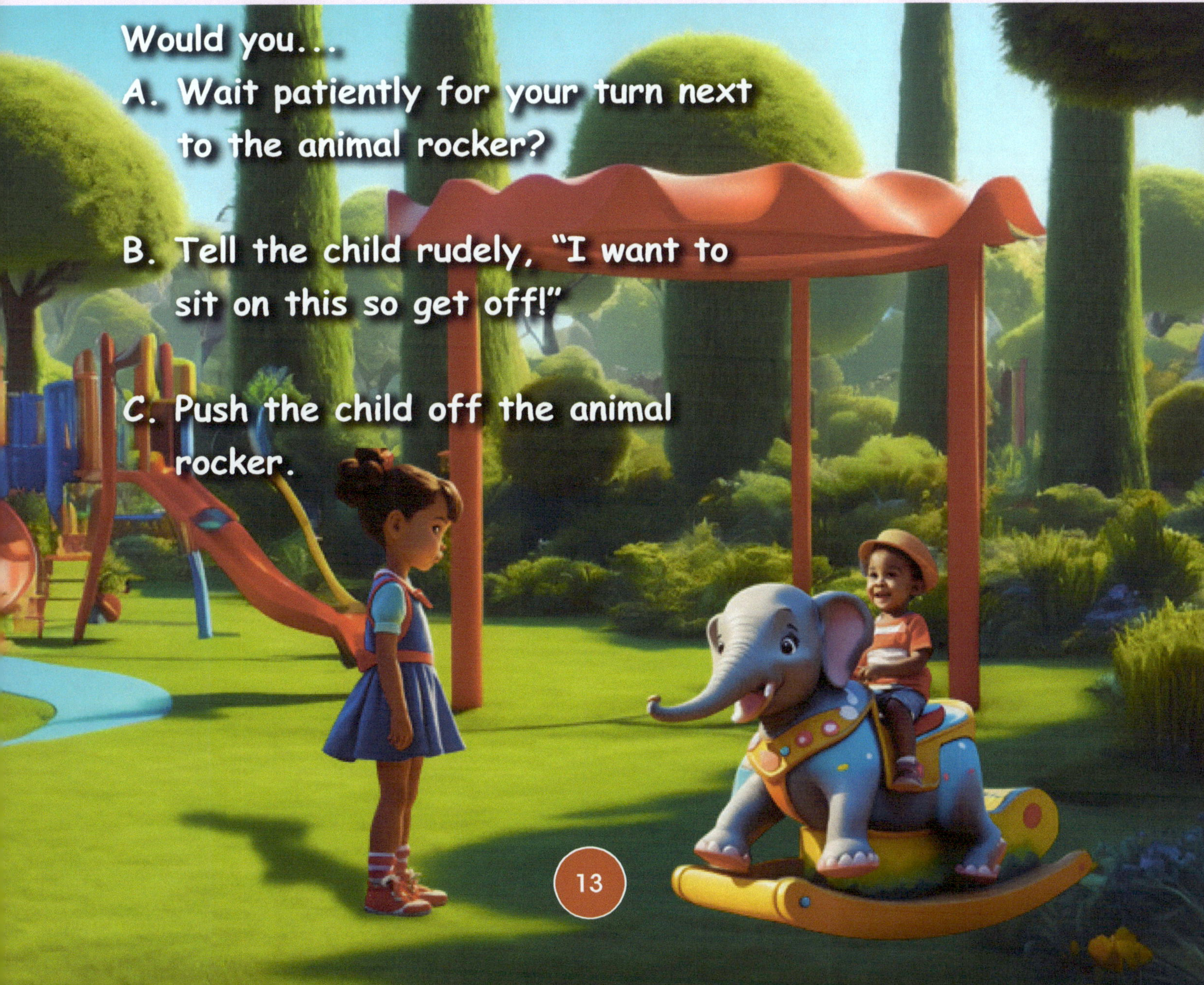

The best thing to do is...

Wait patiently for your turn next to the
animal rocker.

Be patient and respect others.

At School

Supposing the teacher asks a question to your friend, John, the answer to which you know,

Will you...

A. Shout out the right answer?

B. Wait for John to answer?

C. Quietly tell John the correct answer.

17

The best thing to do is to

Wait for John to answer.

It is good to wait for others to take their turn to answer and only answer when it's your turn to.

18

Supposing you are walking in a queue at school. The child behind you pushes you,

Would you...

A. Push the child back?

B. Scream back at the child?

C. Inform the teacher and your parent about the incident.

The best thing to do is to,

Inform the teacher and your parent of the incident.

It is not a good idea to scream or push the child back. We must not reciprocate bad behavior.

20

Supposing you are studying in class and feel like using the restroom,

Would you...

A. Raise your hand and request politely, 'Teacher, May I please use the restroom now?'

B. Start crying and screaming for the Teacher's attention.

C. Wait for the class to be over.

The best thing to do is to raise your hand and request politely,

"Teacher, May I please use the restroom now?"

It is good for your body to use the restroom as soon as you get the feeling.

Shouting and screaming will disturb the entire class.

Supposing you are playing indoors at school with your friends,
And you need a toy that your friend is playing with,

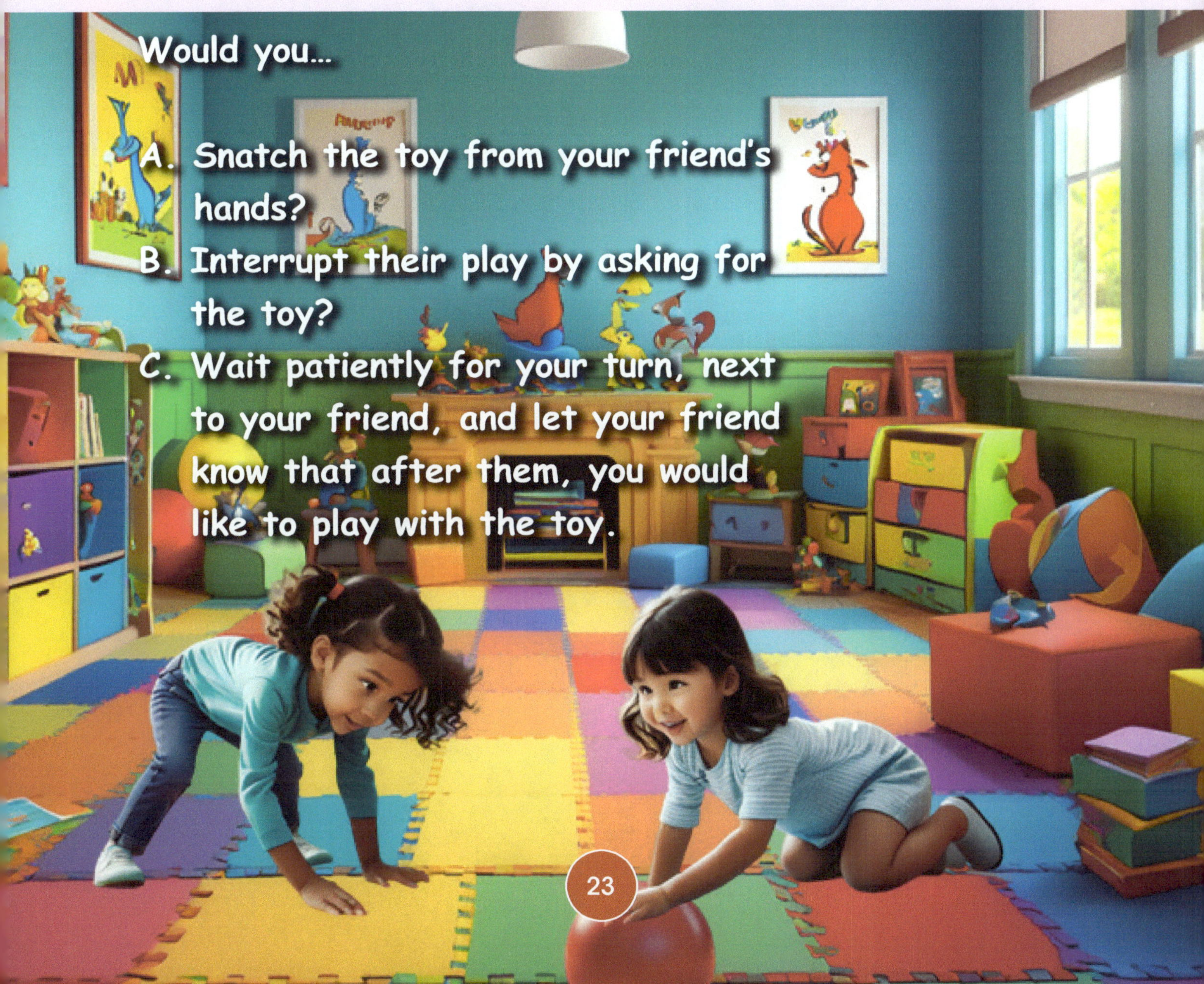

The best thing to do is...

Wait patiently for your turn, next to your friend, and let your friend know that after them, you would like to play with the toy.

Be patient and respect others.

Supposing your friend wins at the school race while you could not....

Will you...

A. Be happy for your friend's achievement and congratulate her?

B. Be angry that you could not win and stop speaking to your friend?

C. Start crying?

25

The best thing to do is to be happy for your friend's achievement and say "Congratulations Lisa, I am so happy for you!"

Sometimes we win and sometimes we don't; we must continue to strive to get better.

Supposing you want to play with a classmate during playtime at school. However, the classmate does not want to play with you...

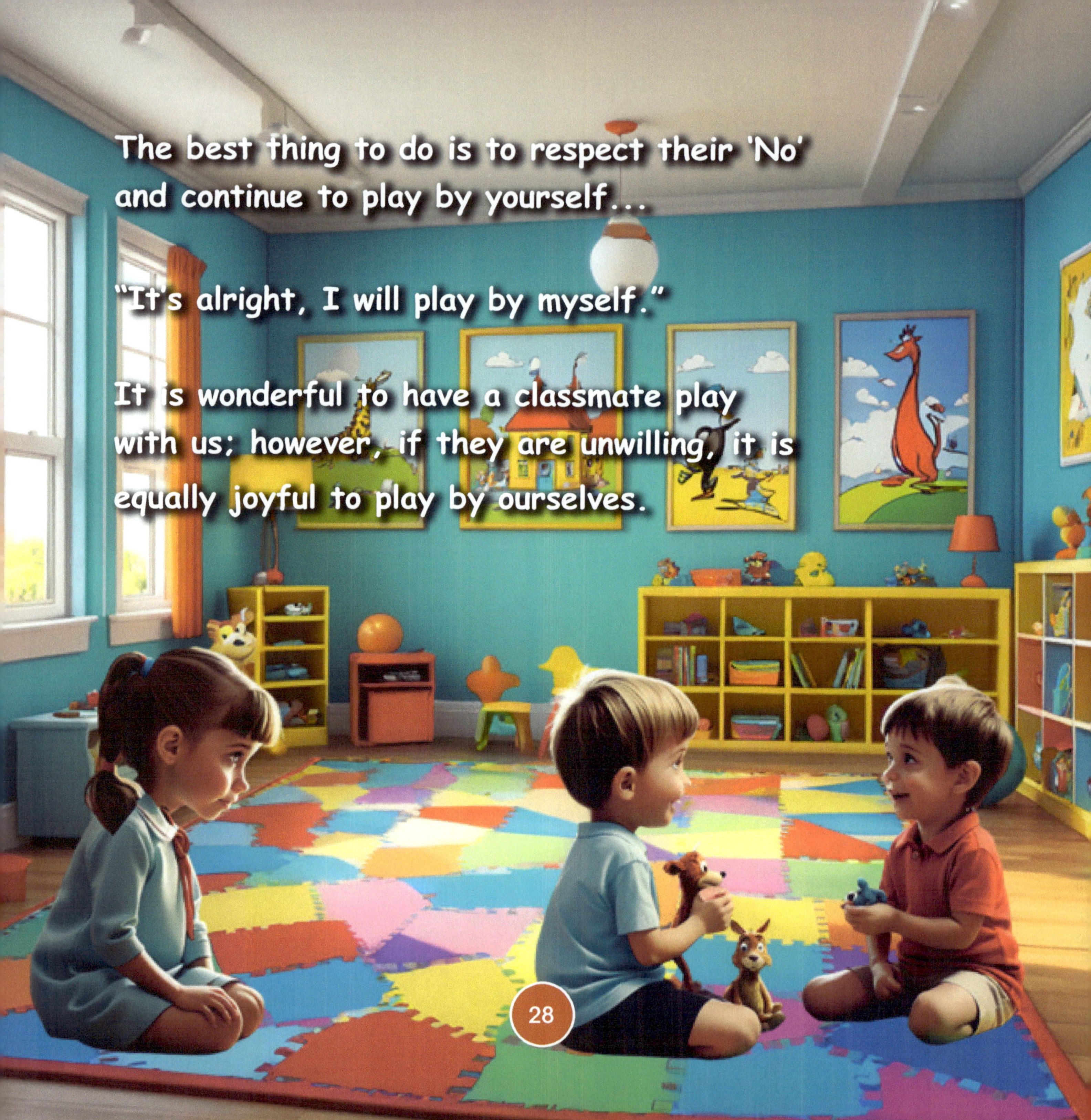
The best thing to do is to respect their 'No'
and continue to play by yourself…

"It's alright, I will play by myself."

It is wonderful to have a classmate play
with us; however, if they are unwilling, it is
equally joyful to play by ourselves.

Supposing you want to use a particular crayon, and your classmate has the same one that you are looking for,

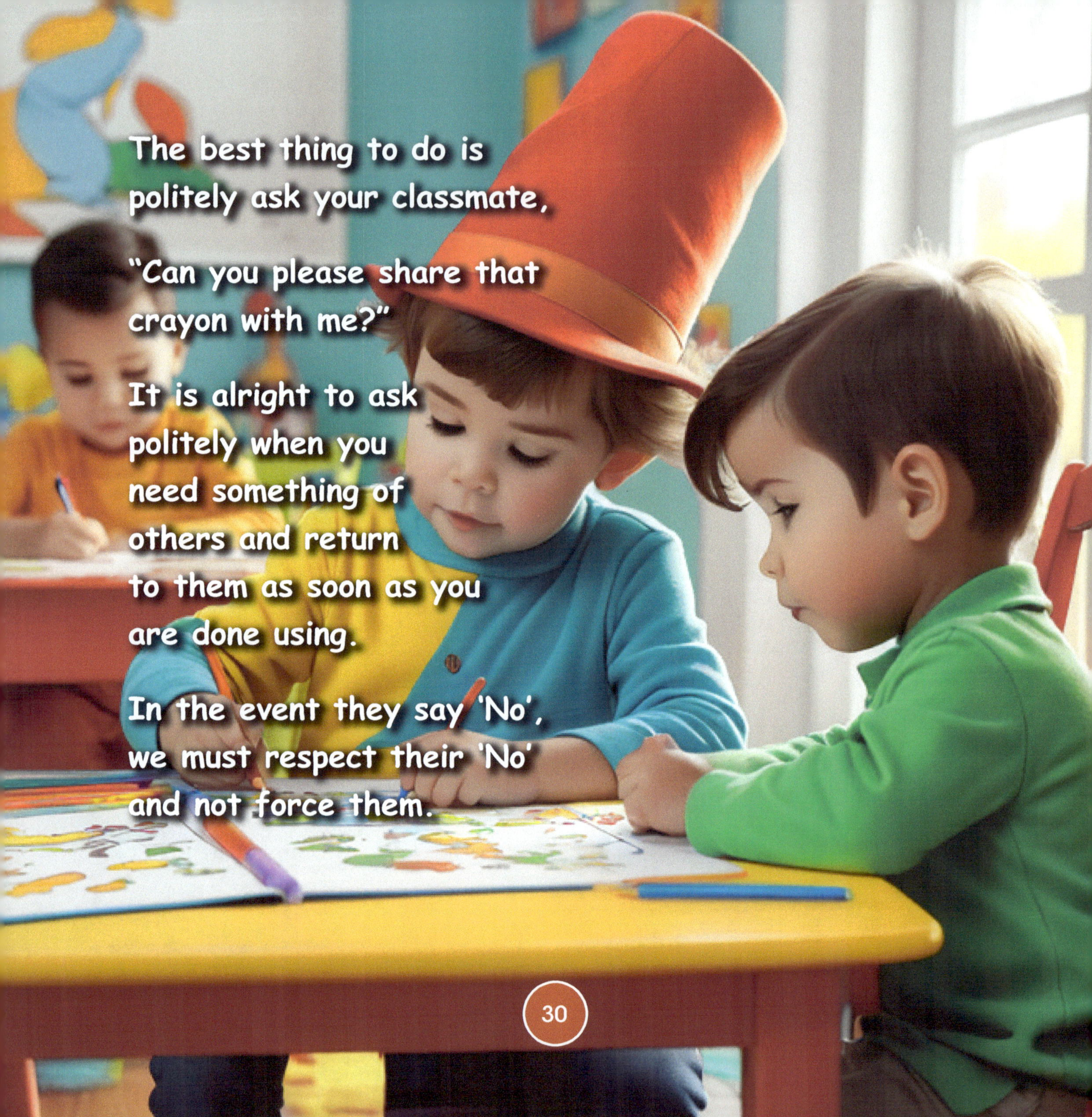

The best thing to do is politely ask your classmate,

"Can you please share that crayon with me?"

It is alright to ask politely when you need something of others and return to them as soon as you are done using.

In the event they say 'No', we must respect their 'No' and not force them.

At Home

Supposing you are playing at home and the doorbell rings. The person insists that you open the door immediately,

The best thing to do is to say politely,

"Please wait,
I would like to call my
Mum or Dad."

Never open the main door for anyone without an elder's supervision, even if you know the person.

Supposing you are eating your meal and need some more rice,

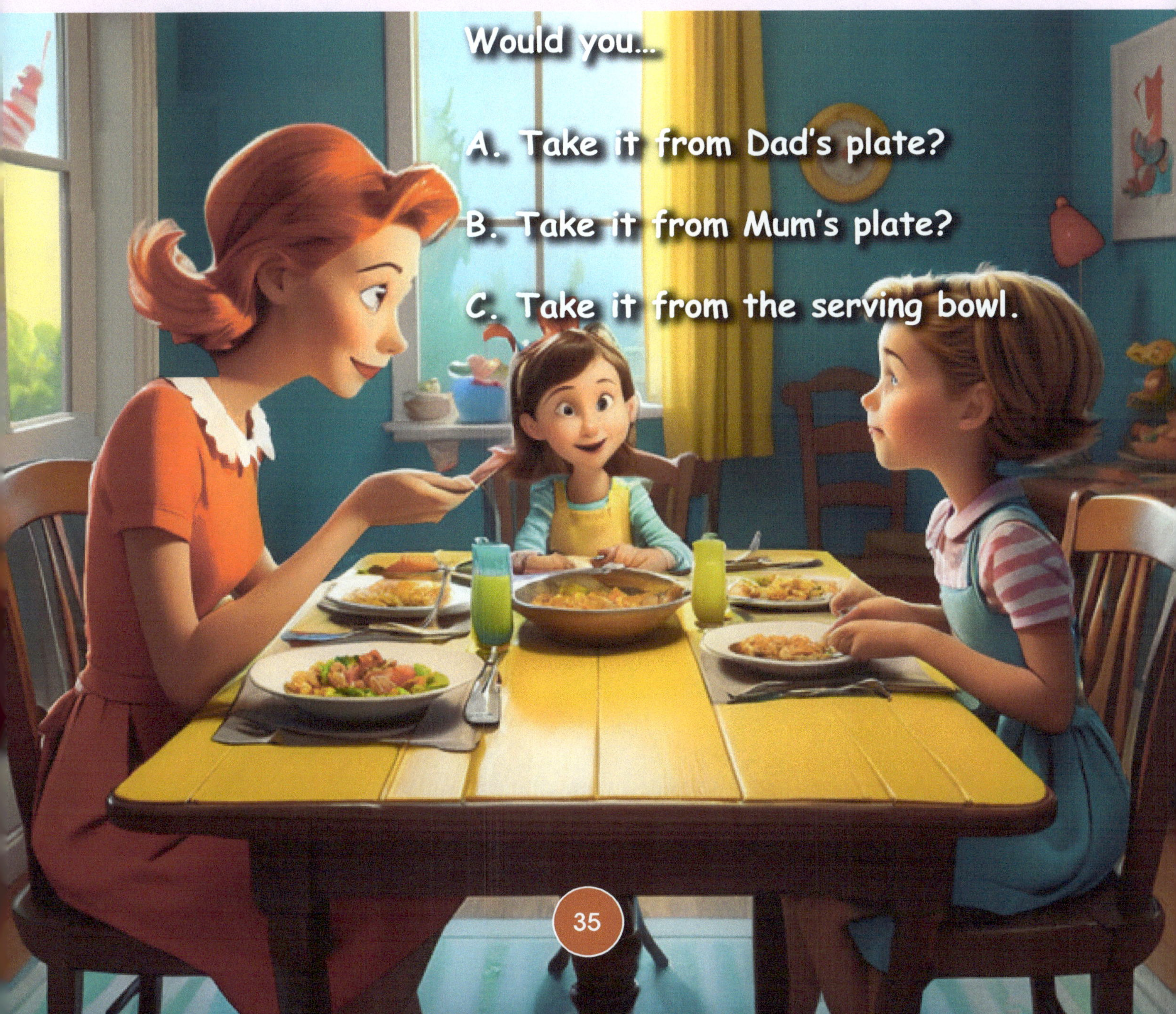

The best thing to do is to,

Take it from the serving bowl.

If you are unable to reach it, you may request your mum or dad to help serve you some more.

It is never a good idea to take food from other people's plates.

36

Supposing an Uncle visits you after a long time and offers you a box of your favourite sweet treats,

The best thing to do is to,

Take one and say "Thank you!"

The Uncle may insist for you to take many
or all. Eating too many sweets may cause
your tummy to ache or lead to cavities.
Hence, we must always eat in moderation.

Supposing you just finished playing with your toys and
your parent calls you for your meal,

Would you...

A. Clean up your toys on your
    own and then go for your meal.

B. Leave your toys as is
    and go for your meal.

C. Expect your mum or dad
    to clean up your toys for you.

39

The best thing to do is to,

Clean up your toys on your
own and then go for your meal.

Cleanliness is next to
Godliness.

40

Supposing you woke up late for School, and your parent requests you to hurry up,

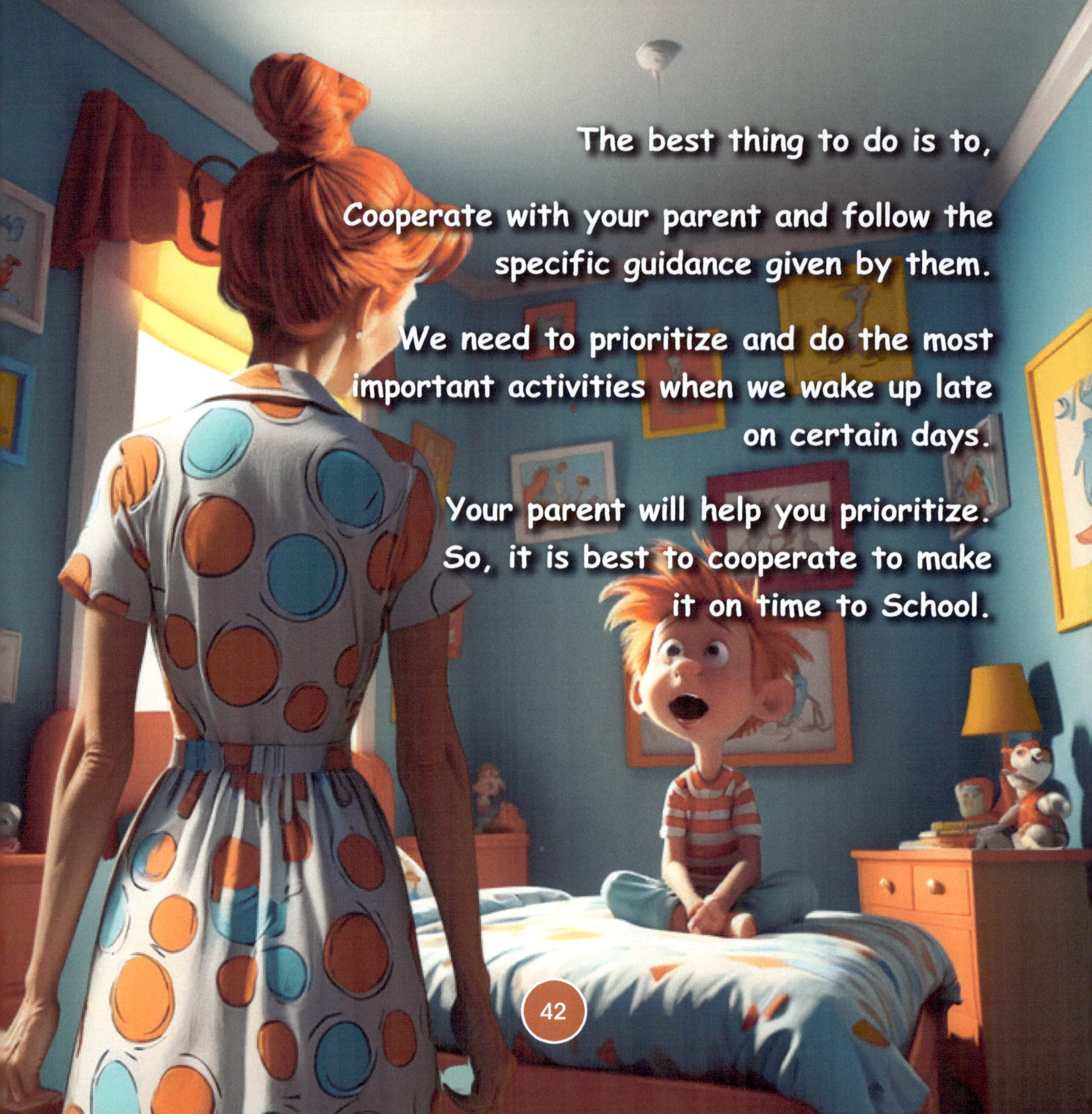

The best thing to do is to,

Cooperate with your parent and follow the specific guidance given by them.

We need to prioritize and do the most important activities when we wake up late on certain days.

Your parent will help you prioritize. So, it is best to cooperate to make it on time to School.

42

Supposing your parent is working from home on their computer,

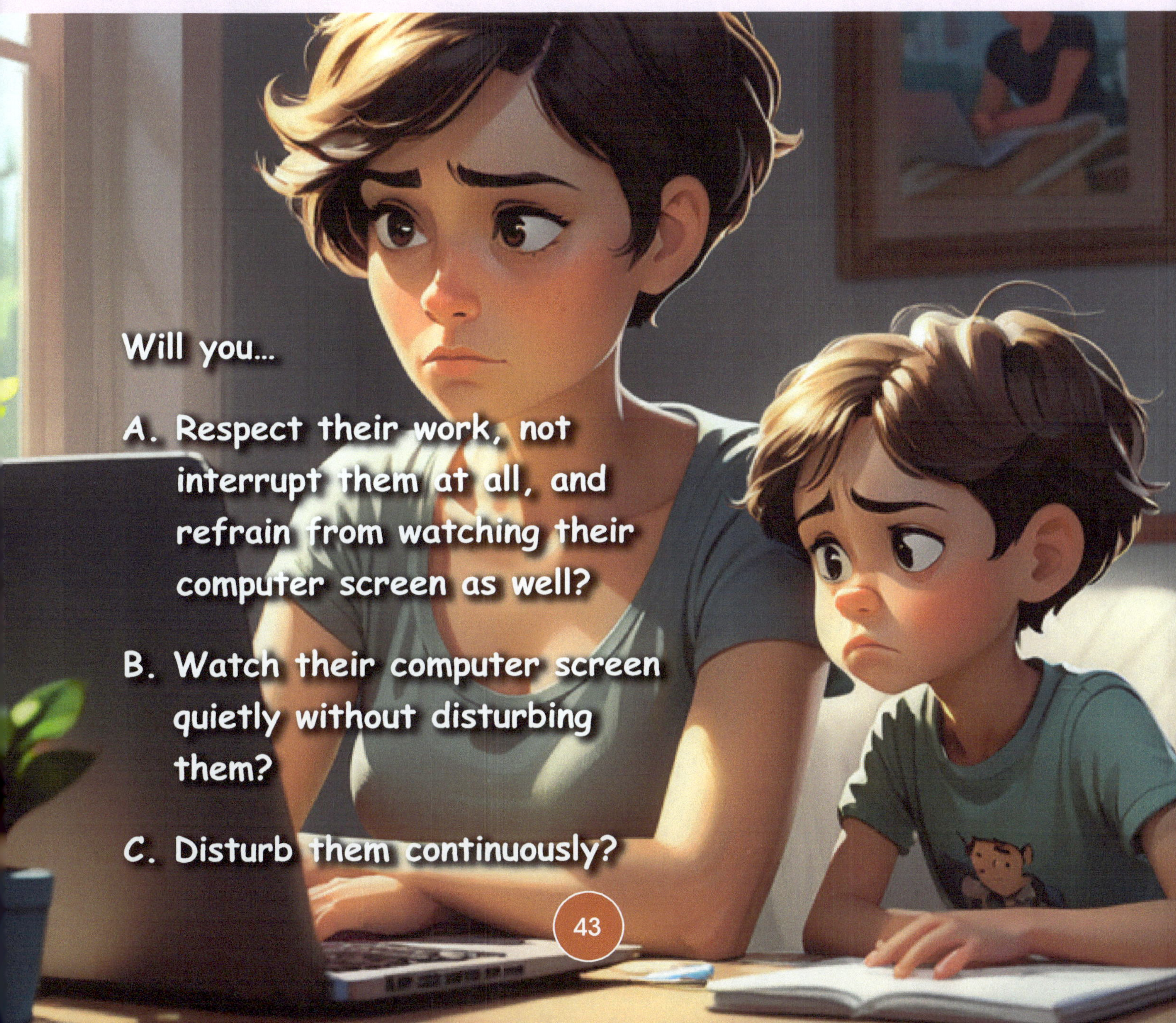

The best thing to do is to respect their work, not interrupt them at all, and refrain from watching their computer screen as well.

Watching the screen for a long time may damage your eyes. Disturbing your parent will cause them to deliver low-quality work, which is not what we want.

We want to support our parents so they succeed at their work.

Will you...

A. Ignore your parent?

B. Clean up what you are doing and head for Homework?

C. Start crying?

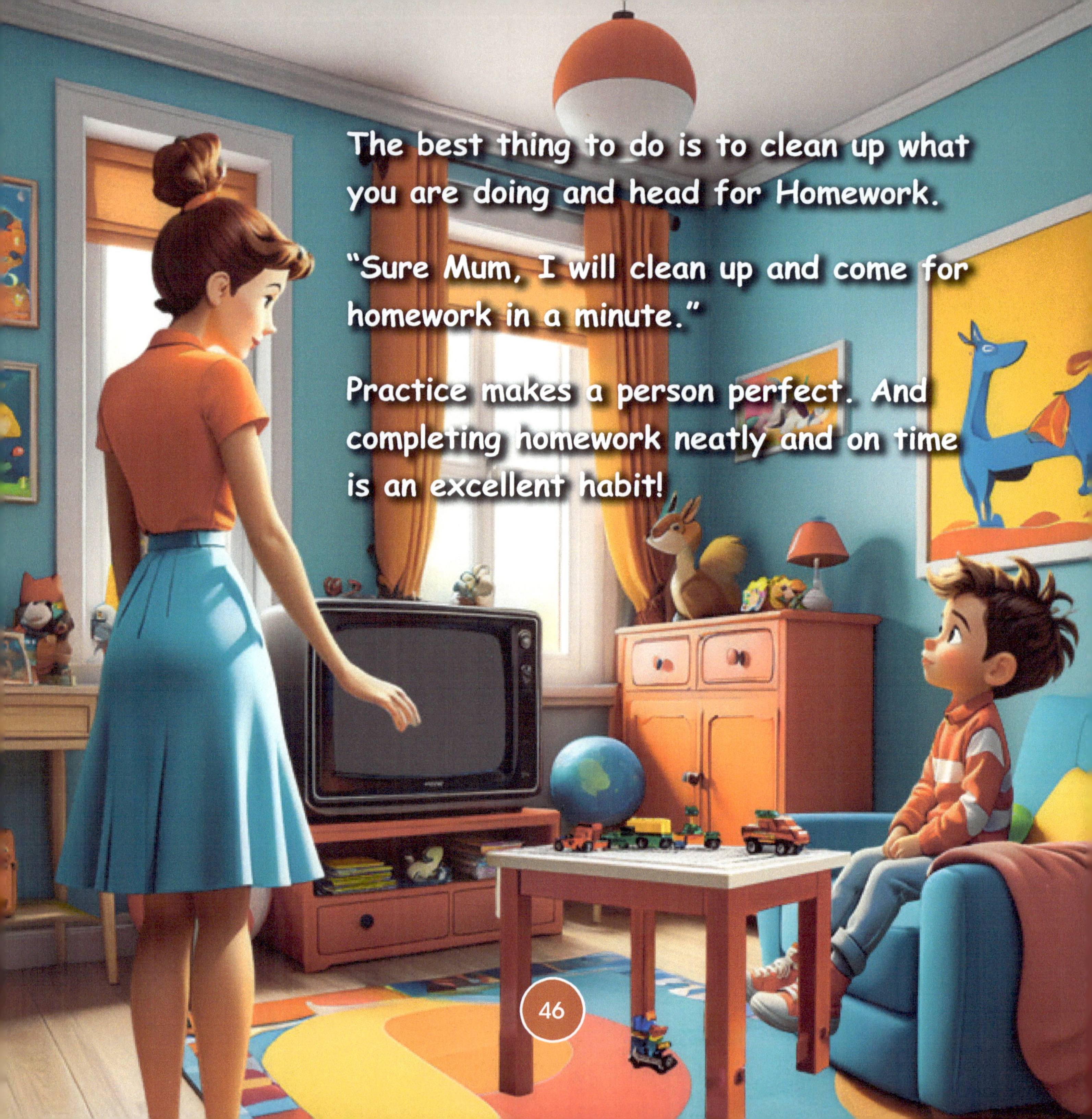

The best thing to do is to clean up what you are doing and head for Homework.

"Sure Mum, I will clean up and come for homework in a minute."

Practice makes a person perfect. And completing homework neatly and on time is an excellent habit!

...